THE TRAILBLAZING LIFE OF

Viola Desmond

A CIVIL RIGHTS ICON

THE TRAILBLAZING LIFE OF

Viola Desmond

A CIVIL RIGHTS ICON

RACHEL KEHOE WITH
WANDA ROBSON

illustrated by
CHELSEA CHARLES

ORCA BOOK PUBLISHERS

To Isla, Rose, Rhys and all the kids whose courage
helps tilt the world the right way.
And to my husband, Bas, for always believing in me.

Text copyright © Rachel Kehoe and Wanda Robson 2023
Illustrations copyright © Chelsea Charles 2023

Published in Canada and the United States in 2023 by Orca Book Publishers.
orcabook.com

Library and Archives Canada Cataloguing in Publication
Title: The trailblazing life of Viola Desmond : a civil rights icon /
Rachel Kehoe with Wanda Robson ; illustrations by Chelsea Charles.
Other titles: Viola Desmond
Names: Kehoe, Rachel, author. | Robson, Wanda, 1926-2022, author. |
Charles, Chelsea, 1994- illustrator.
Description: Includes bibliographical references and index.
Identifiers: Canadiana (print) 20220439222 | Canadiana (ebook) 20220439230 |
ISBN 9781459833975 (hardcover) | ISBN 9781459833982 (PDF) | ISBN 9781459833999 (EPUB)
Subjects: LCSH: Desmond, Viola, 1914-1965—Juvenile literature. | LCSH: Race discrimination—
Nova Scotia—History—Juvenile literature. | LCSH: Civil rights—Nova Scotia—History—Juvenile
literature. | CSH: Black Canadian women—Nova Scotia—Biography—Juvenile literature | CSH: Black
Canadians—Nova Scotia—Biography—Juvenile literature | LCGFT: Biographies.
Classification: LCC FC2346.26.D48 K45 2023 | DDC j971.6/004960092—dc23

Library of Congress Control Number: 2022947220

Summary: This illustrated nonfiction book for middle-grade readers tells the story of
Viola Desmond's life, based on interviews with her sister Wanda Robson.

Orca Book Publishers is committed to reducing the consumption of nonrenewable resources in the
production of our books. We make every effort to use materials that support a sustainable future.

Orca Book Publishers gratefully acknowledges the support for its publishing programs provided by
the following agencies: the Government of Canada, the Canada Council for the Arts and the Province
of British Columbia through the BC Arts Council and the Book Publishing Tax Credit.

Cover and interior artwork by Chelsea Charles
Edited by Kirstie Hudson

Printed and bound in South Korea.

26 25 24 23 • 1 2 3 4

CONTENTS

Introduction

AN ACT OF BRAVERY

On November 19, 2018, Canada issued a new $10 bill. The front shows a picture of the first Black person—and the first woman other than a British royal—to appear alone on Canadian money. Her name is Viola Desmond.

What did she do to earn this?

On November 8, 1946, nine years before Rosa Parks sparked the **civil rights movement** in the United States, Viola took a stand against **racial segregation** in a quiet act of defiance. On that day in 1946, she refused to leave the whites-only section of a theater in New Glasgow, Nova Scotia.

ROSA PARKS

Viola Desmond is often compared to Rosa Parks, the American civil rights icon whose famous act of bravery happened nine years after Viola's protest. On December 1, 1955, Rosa Parks was taking the bus home from work in Montgomery, Alabama. When the bus got crowded, the driver asked the Black passengers in the row behind the "white" section to move back to make room for white passengers boarding. They all got up—except Rosa. Just like Viola, Rosa was not trying to start a movement. She was just fed up with racial discrimination . She wanted the same freedoms as white people. What happened? Rosa was arrested, taken to jail and fined for breaking segregation laws.

But Rosa refused to pay and said the law was wrong. With the help of the Black community, she went to court and accused the bus company of allowing unfair seating rules. Rosa's simple act of protest is seen as the beginning of the civil rights movement in the United States.

At that time in Nova Scotia, Black people and white people lived by different rules. Some restaurants and hotels did not serve Black people. At many theaters and churches, Black people had to sit in separate sections. Canada had officially abolished *slavery* more than 90 years earlier. But Black Canadians still didn't get fair treatment.

Viola's bravery would inspire Black community leaders and blaze a trail for the modern civil rights movement in Canada. She proved that one person could make a difference. Poised, determined and confident, Viola Desmond fought for racial equality and became a symbol of courage to generations of Black Canadians.

It is thanks to Viola's youngest sister, Wanda Robson, that we know her story today. Wanda has worked tirelessly to keep her sister's story alive by giving interviews, speaking with government officials and presenting at universities. Her memories remind us of Viola's bravery and raise awareness of the struggle for **equal rights** in Canada. The stories here were gathered from interviews with Wanda before she died. Wanda is the inspiration for this book, and you will hear her voice in every chapter.

This is Viola's story.

JIM CROW

In the southern United States, Jim Crow laws enforced the separation of Black and white people in schools, neighborhoods and restaurants. They existed for nearly 100 years, from the 1870s until the 1960s. The term Jim Crow came from a popular performance called a minstrel show in the 1800s that mocked Black people. As a result, Jim Crow became a negative way to refer to Black people and, later, the segregation laws that enforced separation from the white population. Although Canada did not have Jim Crow laws like those in the United States, it imposed segregation through court decisions and social practices that limited the freedoms of Black citizens.

On April 15, 2010—Province House, Halifax

As the applause died down, Wanda Robson waited to hear the words that would set her sister free. Sixty-four years earlier, Viola Desmond had carried out a courageous act that fought against racial segregation in Canada. For that she was jailed, convicted and fined. Today the government of Nova Scotia would recognize that this should never have happened. In this case, the law had been wrong.

As then premier Darrell Dexter took the stage, Wanda wished her sister had lived to see this moment. A free **pardon** is granted very rarely. It is based on innocence. It acknowledges that Viola did nothing wrong and that the treatment she received was unfair. "This is a chance for us to finally right the wrong done to Ms. Desmond and her family," said the premier. "This is also an opportunity to acknowledge the incredibly brave actions of a woman who took a stand against **racism** and segregation."

Hearing these words made Wanda go numb with joy. "What happened to my sister is part of our history and needs to remain intact," she said. "We must learn from our history so we do not repeat it." The story of Viola Desmond is one that every Canadian can be proud of. Viola fought for what she believed in and remains a true Canadian hero.

NOTES FROM WANDA

We were a family of civil rights seekers. In 1876 my grandfather, George Davis, fought to desegregate public schools in the North End. He thought it was unfair that all-Black schools were often far away, in run-down buildings with hardly any books or equipment. He knew Black children should be able to attend a school as good as any white one. So he started a petition to do just that. His proposal gathered over 100 signatures, and he succeeded! Black children could go to any public school in the North End. Because of this, his son, Charles Davis, became the first Black student in Halifax to graduate from secondary school.

George didn't stop there. He took an exam and became the first Black postman in Halifax. At the time this was a popular position reserved for white people only. After starting his new job, he gave the family business, the Davis Barber Shop, to his sons. One of them was my father, James.

one

THE DAVIS FAMILY

Viola Davis was born on July 6, 1914. For most of her life she lived in the North End, a Black community in Halifax, Nova Scotia. At the time, it was a bustling neighborhood. Electric trams rumbled along the streets. There were fancy shops filled with elegant dresses, scarves and hats. A theater played the newest silent movies. Ships glided through Halifax Harbour, bringing shipments of steel and coal to the docks.

Viola's family had a long history in Nova Scotia. In the 1800s her ancestors fled slavery in the United States and escaped north to Canada in search of freedom. In Nova Scotia they were no longer slaves, but life was still difficult. Unwritten rules upheld segregation—the separation of Blacks and whites—in communities and public schools. This meant Black people could not live in white neighborhoods or go to the same schools as white children. Businesses refused to serve them, and the only jobs open to Black people, such as construction workers and train porters, paid poorly.

RACIAL HERITAGE

In 1908 Viola's father, James Davis, secretly married Gwendolyn Irene Johnson. Though Gwendolyn looked white, she had a mixed-race heritage and considered herself Black. At the time mixed-race marriages were rare. When Gwendolyn's father found out, he was angry. She was only 19! But he could see that James and Gwendolyn were in love. He even offered James a job. So the couple moved in with James's parents in the North End.

THE UNDERGROUND RAILROAD

The Underground Railroad didn't really run on rails. It was the term for a secret system of routes and hideouts and safe houses that slaves in the southern United States used to escape to freedom in the northern states and Canada. It ran from around 1810 to the 1860s, and some experts say it helped as many as 100,000 Black slaves make the dangerous journey in search of freedom. Enslaved Black people often celebrated their arrival in Canada by shouting they had made it to "heaven."

Soon James and Gwendolyn started a family—a very large family. Viola was the fifth of fifteen children. As often happened back then, four of the children died young. Seven daughters and four sons survived.

At that time children from mixed-race families were considered Black, according to the "one-drop rule." This meant that because Viola's father was Black, she was considered Black too.

FAMILY MATTERS

In 1915 Viola became a big sister when Hazel Davis was born. However, this joy was followed by great sadness when two-year-old Hazel contracted pneumonia, a disease that made it difficult for her to breathe. She died from it. Shortly afterward Viola came down with the same illness. She became so sick the doctor didn't think she would survive. Viola recovered, but her parents worried about her. Viola was small for her age. She had a quiet voice, and though she was a bright and curious child, everything about her seemed fragile. Whenever the children went out together,

THE HALIFAX EXPLOSION

This is one of the worst disasters in Canadian history. It happened shortly after 9:00 a.m. on December 6, 1917. Just as people were going to work and children were walking to school, the *Imo*, a Norwegian supply ship, collided with the *Mont-Blanc*, a French cargo vessel carrying **munitions**. The *Mont-Blanc*, burning fiercely, drifted into a pier on the Halifax shoreline and exploded. The blast sent up a huge fireball. White-hot shards of iron flew through the air. The disaster left 2,000 people dead and 9,000 injured. Nearly 12,000 homes were destroyed, and every building within 12 miles (20 kilometers) was damaged.

their father would remind them, "Take care of Viola—you know she's delicate." Her brothers and sisters always looked out for her, but they knew she was tougher than she looked.

When she was three years old, Viola had another close call. She was sitting by the window in her high chair when an explosion shook the house. Broken glass rained down over her body, and the window blind fell on her head. Viola was so quiet that her father thought she had been killed. When he lifted the blind, he found her unhurt. The Halifax Explosion shattered the city. The North End was one of the hardest-hit areas.

After the explosion, Viola's family moved four blocks away to a house on John Street. They spent several happy years there. Everyone worked hard and had chores. Viola's older sisters, Helen and Emily, helped their mother with the cooking while brothers Henry and Gordon brought in coal for the stove. Because she was small, Viola usually got the easier jobs. Sometimes her siblings would get annoyed that all she had to do was set the table and clear the plates. But this never bothered Viola.

When she wasn't helping out, Viola loved to read. Her parents' house had so many books, it looked like a library. Often she climbed into her favorite rocking chair with a book. She was eager to learn and discover new things.

LESSONS IN COLOR LINES

Faith was an important part of Viola's childhood. Every Sunday her family got dressed in their best clothes. They walked two blocks to the Trinity Anglican Church.

At Trinity, the Davises were one of very few Black families. Most Black people were members of the Baptist church that had started because Blacks were not welcome at other white churches. But Viola's father was proud of his Anglican faith. Nonetheless, the family never felt as though they belonged. The children were never invited to church picnics or included at parties.

This "color line," the separation of white and Black people, also existed at school. In the Davis household, education was everything. Gwendolyn, Viola's mother, said, "They can take anything from you...but they can't take your education." Viola attended Joseph Howe Elementary, where her classes included both Black and white students. Viola was one of the smartest girls in class. She had a good memory and performed well on exams. However, teachers gave more help and attention to white students. Many educators at the time thought a Black student would not achieve as much.

But Viola wasn't bothered by what other people thought. She knew if she worked hard, she could achieve the same as any white child. And she would prove it.

NOTES FROM WANDA

Viola loved to read and learn. But she hated to cook. She enjoyed making only one thing: seven-minute frosting. Today it's easy to make with an electric mixer. But back then it was considered a skill. The ingredients had to be mixed with a hand beater. Viola would pour in the ingredients—egg whites, sugar and vanilla—and whisk everything together for seven minutes. It was tough work. Some women had to take turns, but Viola would stand there and whip up the most delicious icing. I think the main reason she liked to make icing was so she could lick the beater.

two

A FAIR EDUCATION

At Bloomfield High School, Viola was a top student. She excelled in history, English and geography. Viola made sure her work was neat and her answers correct.

It was in her nature to be precise. This went beyond the classroom. Viola had tidy hair, clean nails and stylish clothes. She always looked immaculate.

Viola could often be serious, but she also knew how to have fun. She enjoyed music and loved singing with her sisters. Viola's younger sister Olive would start singing in the kitchen and Viola would join in, adding harmony. Music filled the house. Her parents also had a Victrola, one of the first record players. The children loved to wind the handle, roll up the rug and dance.

HARD TIMES

In 1929, when Viola was 15 years old, the **Great Depression** struck. It was driven by a stock market crash around the world. Businesses failed, and millions of Canadians lost their jobs. At the same time, there was a drought that wiped out crops in the prairies. Food became scarce, and people were hungry. In the cities people stood in food lines to get handouts of soup and bread.

Viola's father, James, could only find occasional work washing cars. The job did not pay well. One night the family sat down to dinner. Gwendolyn turned from the stove with tears in her eyes. She served the children a bit of porridge and a piece of dry toast. Viola's brother complained, "We had this for breakfast."

James sat down. "This is what we have tonight," he said. "This is all we have."

He felt horrible that he could not look after his family. He felt worse when they had to take their son Henry out of school to work. Luckily, Henry got a job as a chauffeur for Graham Dennis, the newspaperman who owned the *Chronicle Herald*. The money he made was enough to help out with food, clothes and rent.

SCHOOLING IN TRURO

Viola's parents had always taught their children to work hard. Now it was Viola's turn to show them what she could achieve. She graduated from high school in 1930 at the age of 16 and dreamed of becoming a teacher. But it wouldn't be easy. Opportunities for

Black women to become teachers were minimal, and the teachers college in Truro did not admit Black people. And even if Viola could get a teaching certificate, she would only be allowed to teach at segregated Black elementary schools. To teach in them, Viola would need to pass a provincial exam.

But Viola was determined to become a teacher. What's more, she wanted to attend a teachers college, just like any white student could. Even though the odds were against her, Viola submitted her application to the teachers college in Truro. On the form was a box that asked for her race. Because of her answer, she was rejected.

But Viola didn't give up.

Although she couldn't attend college, she applied to take the provincial exam to earn her teaching certificate, even though it would qualify her to work only at segregated schools. At age 19 she began working at segregated schools in North Preston and Hammonds Plains near Halifax. Compared to the nearest white schools, the places where Viola taught were run-down. There were never enough books or blackboards. But none of this mattered to Viola. She set high standards for her students. She wouldn't let them limit their ambitions just because fewer opportunities existed for Black people.

Viola also took an interest in the education of her younger siblings. She helped them with their homework and taught them how to read and write. But, more important, she encouraged them to have a sense of pride and self-confidence. Her sister Wanda remembers that whenever she felt the sting of racism, Viola encouraged her to "be strong" and "speak her mind."

Viola believed in standing up for herself. She stood up for her students as well. And if her family needed her, she stood up for them too.

NOTES FROM WANDA

When I was seven or eight years old, I had a friend, Marjory, who lived across the street from me. We got along really well and loved playing games out in the backyard. Marjory's dad was in the army. Whenever he came home, Marjory wasn't allowed to come out and play with me, and I wasn't allowed to come over to her house. One day I asked her why and Marjory explained, "My dad told me we couldn't play together." My own father was very annoyed when he heard this. He didn't want me to play with Marjory anymore. But my mother and Viola were more understanding. They knew we were just kids who didn't see skin color as a big deal. "They're friends and they don't understand it, so let them play as little girls," my mother said.

three

EQUAL FROM FROM THE START

RUBY BRIDGES

Ruby Bridges was the first Black student to attend an all-white elementary school in the southern United States. On November 14, 1960, when Ruby was six years old, federal marshals escorted her to William Frantz Elementary School in New Orleans. Screaming protesters crowded the pavement and tried to block the entrance. They were angry because they didn't want Ruby at their school. On her first day, Ruby and her mother sat in the principal's office. They watched as the parents of white kids came in throughout the day to remove their kids from school. Some were scared of the protesters. Others didn't want their children to *integrate*.

With 12 years' difference between them, Viola was like a mother to her sister Wanda. Viola would do her sister's hair and they would talk.

When she entered the second grade, Wanda enrolled at a new school called Alexandra Elementary School, a nonsegregated school in the North End of Halifax. She was so excited for her first day. But when Wanda returned home, Viola could tell something wasn't right. Then, a few weeks later, Wanda came home from school in tears. Viola knew Wanda had loved first grade and was a good student. What had happened?

Through gulping sobs, Wanda told Viola and her mother everything that had happened. On the very first day of school, her teacher, Ms. Reid, had sent her to sit at the back with the other Black students. "She completely ignored us," said Wanda.

"The only time she noticed us was when we made a noise and she told us to be quiet." No matter how hard Wanda tried, Ms. Reid never called on her or let her ask any questions.

Viola was shocked. She couldn't imagine treating students so unfairly.

Then Wanda told her sister that Ms. Reid had one rule: the kids who got top marks could sit in the front row. "I listened and worked hard," said Wanda. "On the next exam, I got the highest mark in the class, and Ms. Reid moved me to the front."

But somehow things only got worse.

Wanda could sense that Ms. Reid was upset with her. She stayed angry the whole day and even seemed frustrated with the other Black students.

"I kept doing well on my tests, and I stayed at the front." Wanda's eyes welled up as she told Viola the story. "But a few days later, Ms. Reid was still mad. She got angry every time I raised my hand."

UNFAIR PUNISHMENT

Ms. Reid had had enough of Wanda. The next time Wanda raised her hand, she said, "Oh look, we have a genius in our class—a girl who knows everything. So what do we do with people who are too smart for this class? We put them in the next class." Ms. Reid took Wanda to the third-grade teacher. Wanda heard her teacher say, "This is Wanda Davis. She's in our class, and she is to go to the back of your room. Don't give her anything to do. Just make her sit there and think about how she's showing off in class."

By now Wanda was crying. The third-grade teacher felt sorry for her and told her to continue with her lessons while in her class. Wanda felt confused. What had she done wrong? After a few weeks Wanda was returned to her old class. But again Ms. Reid sent her right to the back of the room. But the next day was Parents' Day, and Wanda was upset because she hadn't told everybody what had happened. "I'm sorry I got in trouble," Wanda said. "I just don't know what to do."

As Viola listened, her lips pressed into a thin line. The following day Viola and her mother went to visit Ms. Reid. Both Davis women had the same temperament. They didn't get angry, and they never yelled. Viola's mother had taught her that with poise, determination and courage, she would always succeed.

The day after the meeting, Wanda was pleased to find herself placed back at the front of the room. Viola told Wanda that she hadn't done anything wrong. "You earned your place at the front of the room and that is where you should sit," Viola told her. Viola wasn't about to let Ms. Reid's prejudice hold her sister back. She wanted her sister to feel proud of who she was.

INSPIRING CHANGE

Meanwhile Viola was starting to wonder about her own future. She had read an article about Madam C.J. Walker, a Black **beautician** and self-made millionaire. She owned a chain of beauty salons in the United States. Madam Walker's talent and success inspired Viola. At the time there were almost no Black beauty salons in Canada. If a Black woman tried going to a salon to have her hair done, she would be refused.

Viola showed the article to her friend and schoolmate Portia White. "I want to do that," she said.

"Well, go ahead and do it," said Portia.

So Viola made a decision that changed the rest of her life. She would become a beautician.

MADAM C.J. WALKER

The daughter of slaves, Madam C.J. Walker was working as a domestic helper when she began to lose her hair. Desperate for her hair to grow back, she invented a mixture to use on her scalp. It worked! In 1905 she started her own business, selling specialized hair products for Black women. Her company hired thousands of door-to-door saleswomen from across the United States. By 1916 the *New York Times* declared her one of the most successful Black female **entrepreneurs** in the United States. Before she died in 1919, Madam Walker was known as the first American woman to become a self-made millionaire.

Is Your Hair Short?
Breaking Off, Thin, or Falling Out?
C. J. WALKER
The Mme. C. J.
Walker Mfg. Co.
640 N. West St., Indianapolis, Ind.

NOTES FROM WANDA

When Viola started her business, there wasn't a single Black beautician working in Halifax. If you were Black and went to a beauty shop, you were turned away. I was denied service at a hairdresser in the 1970s. I entered the shop and was told abruptly by one of the hairdressers, "We don't do you people's hair." So when Vi's Studio of Beauty Culture opened, it was a big deal. Right from the start, her salon attracted many customers. Some were even famous. Gwen Jenkins, who visited Vi's Children's Club when she was just a girl, went on to become the first Black nurse in Nova Scotia. Carrie Best was a civil rights activist, and Portia White was an internationally renowned opera singer. Viola's salon became a popular weekend hangout. The ladies enjoyed Viola's positive and supportive nature.

four

CHASING
A DREAM

In the 1920s, beauty schools in Halifax did not accept Black women. Once again, like the teachers colleges Viola had applied to, these places were for white students only. Viola was frustrated. She longed to be a beautician. But how could she if there weren't any schools to train her?

Viola began to research beauty schools in other provinces. She came across the Field Beauty Culture School in Montreal. It was a small school on St. Antoine Street. She wrote to the instructor, Maud Field, and received a positive response. Viola felt a spark of hope. But Montreal was 775 miles (1,250 kilometers) away. Tuition plus a train ticket would be expensive.

So Viola kept teaching and saving her money. It took nearly three years. Once she had enough money set aside, she sent in her application. Viola was accepted. In 1936, at age 22, she boarded a train to Montreal. The train journey took nearly 24 hours. It was the farthest she had ever been from home.

Right before she left, Viola met Jack Desmond. He was the first registered Black barber in Halifax and owner of Jack's Barbershop in the North End. It was a popular place for locals and

THE COLOR LINE CONFIRMED

In July 1936 Fred Christie was denied service at the York Tavern in Montreal because he was Black. Fred took legal action and brought his case to the Supreme Court. In 1939 the court ruled that the bar had the right to deny service based on skin color.

visiting servicemen coming in off ships. The pair met at a dance at the Gerrish Street Hall, where Jack impressed Viola with his modern moves. Together they danced the jitterbug and waltz.

In many ways they were different. Where Viola was elegant and tenacious, Jack was laid-back and loved to entertain. His outgoing personality earned him the nickname "King of Gottingen Street." Both believed in hard work and shared the same interest in owning a business. Jack admired Viola for her dedication to becoming a trained beautician. He knew she was intelligent and determined. They continued to date while she was away at the Field Beauty Culture School.

Viola was thrilled to be in Montreal. It was a huge, modern city. Skyscrapers stretched high into the sky. An ice rink seated 9,300 spectators. Automobiles swarmed the streets, and the first commercial flights took off from the city's international airport.

In other ways, Montreal was just like Halifax. Black people lived in segregated neighborhoods and often struggled to find well-paying jobs. Restaurants, cinemas and stores still regularly refused Black customers.

NEW BEGINNINGS

Viola had been at school for a few months when Jack decided to make a trip to Montreal to visit her. They were so excited to see each other that during his trip Jack proposed. Before Viola graduated, they got married in Montreal in front of a Baptist minister.

WOMEN HELPING WOMEN

Annie Malone was an early *pioneer* of Black hair care. She was born in 1869 on a farm in Illinois to parents who were former slaves. In high school Annie took an interest in chemistry. She was often ill, however, and was not able to graduate. Annie combined her love of chemistry with her sister's interest in herbal medicine. Together they invented Wonderful Hair Grower, a shampoo that could straighten hair and heal damaged scalps. At the time many women used bacon grease and goose fat as hair straighteners. These harsh methods did a lot of damage to Black hair. Annie patented her shampoo under the name Poro and went on to develop other products that would transform hair care for Black Americans.

Viola returned to Halifax's North End in 1937. Now a trained beautician, she opened Vi's Studio of Beauty Culture on the bottom floor of her parents' house. It was the first hairdressing salon for Black women in Halifax. And an instant success!

She offered various services, including cutting and styling hair for girls going to proms and dances. In addition, she opened Vi's Children's Club, where children could have their hair washed and braided.

Viola was passionate about people and cared about her customers. The younger women looked up to her. Viola took them under her wing and was like a mother to them all.

Viola was living her dream. But really, she was just getting started.

NOTES FROM WANDA

No matter how busy Viola got with her salon, she continued to update her skills. In 1941 she went to New York to complete a course in wig making. I can tell you it is a detailed and time-consuming process! But Viola's work was perfect. When she returned to Halifax she taught our mother how to make wigs so she could have a more relaxing job.

I worked for Viola too. I got paid 50 cents a week to bring supplies back to the salon. I filled the cans of pomade and put Viola's picture on the label. Naturally Viola wanted to make sure everything was done just right. She bought a pair of weighing scales to measure each product and said, "If you are going to weigh for me, you need to be precise. I don't shortchange my customers."

five

BLACK BEAUTY CULTURE COMES TO CANADA

Viola was proud of her business. She loved to help women feel confident about their appearance. But she wanted to do more. Some of her clients had started asking her about particular problems. What should they do with hair that didn't grow or that broke off? Viola listened to their concerns. She wanted to find solutions. So she decided to go back to school.

In 1939 Viola went to the Apex College of Beauty Culture and Hairdressing in Atlantic City, New Jersey. It specialized in teaching students to use a range of Black beauty products such as hot combs, pomades and pressing oils. She trained a girl she could trust, Rose Gannon, to help run the salon in Halifax while she was away.

In Atlantic City, Viola wore the Apex uniform. It was an apron-style skirt and white cap. She trained under the school's founder, Madam Sara Spencer Washington, who was famous for her beauty products and beauty schools in the United States.

STRENGTH AND BEAUTY

Viola updated her skills many times over the years. By 1942 Viola had moved her studio to a larger place on Gottingen Street. She used the back room to make her own line of beauty products under the brand name Sepia. Viola sold face powder, hair dye, perfume and lipstick. Her products included Sur Gro for hair growth, Press Oil for straightening and Gloss Wax for shine.

MADAM SARA SPENCER WASHINGTON

Madam Sara Spencer Washington's empire included laboratories, drugstores and a publishing company that supplied beauty information. In 1913 she opened her own small hairdressing shop in Atlantic City. Madam Washington worked in the shop during the day and sold her hair products door to door at night. By the mid-1930s, her line included 70 products, and she had opened 12 beauty schools in cities throughout the United States.

Viola began traveling around the province to deliver her merchandise and provide hairdressing services to a growing clientele. She learned how to drive, got a license and bought herself a Dodge sedan. Back then it was unusual for a woman to drive her own car and work outside the home. But Viola was different. She was ambitious and independent and believed that the beauty needs of

Black women deserved attention. She dreamed of expanding her business throughout Canada.

Viola believed that Black women should have equal training opportunities too. So in 1944 she established the Desmond School of Beauty Culture. It was the first school of its kind in

Canada, and it opened a whole new world of career opportunities for Black women.

The school graduated five students in 1944. The following year enrollment grew to 15 students, who came from Nova Scotia, New Brunswick and Quebec. Viola wanted to create an image of Black women as beautiful, successful and chic. She told students who completed their training that "as graduates, you are women who know who you are."

In her own way, Viola wanted to prove that Black women were just as good as anyone else. She had made it this far. But there was still so much left she wanted to do.

BLACK HAIR CARE

In the early 1900s it became fashionable for Black women to straighten their naturally tight curls. But its unique texture made their hair especially fragile and susceptible to damage from hot combs used for straightening. The process would often result in burns, *scalp lesions* and hair loss. As a result many women turned to hairpieces and wigs as a way to have straighter hair without the painful procedure. Today there is a growing trend among Black women to choose hairstyles that promote healthy hair, such as braids, twists and *dreadlocks*.

NOTES FROM WANDA

When Viola told me what happened to her
at the movie theater, I became sure of one
thing: I could not have done what Viola did.
I would have left the theater. At 19 years old,
I wasn't the type of person to speak out. I had
a good job, got along with everybody and
did well. I didn't want to rock the boat. At the
time, there was a lot of discussion about what
happened to Viola. I overheard one person
at my work say, "Who did she think she was,
that she couldn't go upstairs?" I just ignored
it. I knew a few colleagues who would have
preferred not to work with me because I was
Black. But I was lucky to have a boss who
didn't see color. And the people around me
were good friends. I knew I had the kind of
world few Black people had, and I wanted to
protect it. I didn't want to be connected with
anything racist. It would only mean trouble.

six

SHE WILL NOT BE MOVED

It was a cold, drizzly morning on November 8, 1946, when Viola said goodbye to her clients at Vi's Studio and set out to make a delivery of beauty products to the city of Sydney on Cape Breton Island.

Everything was going well until, partway through her trip, her car engine started to make strange noises. The town of New Glasgow was up ahead. Viola decided to stop at the closest service station and ask for help. The mechanic told her he would have to order a new part. Her car wouldn't be ready until the following morning.

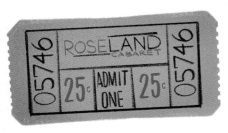

Realizing she was stuck in New Glasgow for the evening, Viola tried to stay calm. She would just have to make her delivery the next day. But she wasn't used to having free time. What should she do?

Viola walked down the main street of New Glasgow and noticed the movie *The Dark Mirror* was playing at the Roseland Theatre. It starred Olivia de Havilland, one of her favorite actresses. Viola rarely had time to watch movies back in Halifax. Why not? she thought.

She walked into the theater and told the cashier, "I'll have a ticket for downstairs, please." At that time patrons could choose to watch a movie from the downstairs section or the balcony. A

downstairs ticket was more expensive, but Viola had bad eyesight, so she liked to sit close to the screen.

Viola entered the main floor and sat down on the lower level. She stretched out her legs and started to relax as the opening credits played. It felt good to be warm.

All of a sudden she felt a tap on her shoulder. It was the usher.

"Miss, you can't sit here," he told her.

"Well, why not?" asked Viola.

"Your ticket is for the balcony upstairs," he explained.

There must be some mistake, Viola thought. She would go back to the cashier and get herself a downstairs ticket.

UNCOMMON COURAGE

Back at the desk, Viola handed over the extra money and said, "I'd like a ticket for downstairs, please." But as Viola spoke, she saw the cashier's face harden. She looked at Viola and said,

"I'm not allowed to sell downstairs tickets to you people."

Viola shivered as the words hit home. *Not allowed. You people.* The cashier hadn't mentioned anything about Viola being Black. But Viola understood what she meant. The downstairs section was for white people only.

Viola was no stranger to racism. She served other Black women every day and knew what life was like for them in Halifax. Black girls could not go into nursing, and they could not have their hair washed or curled in beauty parlors in Halifax. She had also experienced it herself over the years but had always tried to make the best of it. Yet here she was, a successful businesswoman who had built her own career, and still all they saw was the color of her skin.

Frustrated, Viola placed the extra money on the counter. "I am going to sit downstairs because I am short, my eyesight is not good, and I always sit downstairs in a movie theater," she said.

RACIAL SEGREGATION IN NOVA SCOTIA

At first Viola didn't know she had entered a racially segregated movie theater. The practice of racial segregation was different from place to place throughout Nova Scotia. Sometimes the rules were different even within the same community. For example, if Viola had crossed the main street of New Glasgow and gone to the Academy Theatre, she would have found the segregated seating opposite to Roseland Theatre's—Black people had to sit downstairs, and white people sat upstairs.

Viola walked down the aisle, back to her downstairs seat. The movie was just beginning. Once again she tried to get comfortable. Within a minute the usher returned. "Miss, you really can't sit here. If you don't move, I will have to call the manager," he said.

Viola prided herself on behaving politely. But this time she refused to give in and comply. "I am not doing anything wrong. You can call the manager," Viola said.

Henry MacNeil arrived. But Viola wouldn't budge. "I am not causing any trouble," she said. "I offered the cashier the difference in pay. I have to sit downstairs."

"You have been told you can't sit here. If you don't move, I will have to call a policeman," warned Henry.

"Well, get a policeman," said Viola. "I am doing nothing wrong." Henry came back with a policeman and asked, "For the last time, are you going to move?"

"No." Viola's voice was quiet but firm. "I am not moving."

UNNECESSARY ROUGHNESS

The policeman took one arm, and Henry took the other. Together they dragged Viola roughly up the aisle, wrenching her hip. Viola dropped her purse, and one of her shoes was yanked off.

On her way out Viola grabbed on to the sides of the door. She later told her sister Wanda it was because "I wasn't going willingly." Both men had to pry her fingers loose to get her outside.

One woman sitting in the downstairs section of the theater ran up the aisle behind her. She looked at Viola in distress and said, "Oh dear, oh dear," as she gave back the shoe and purse.

Frightened and bruised, Viola was driven to the local jail.

She couldn't believe what was happening. All she had wanted was to keep her seat and watch a movie. And now she was in jail. As she entered her cell, Viola kept thinking, What is happening? What have I done wrong?

NOTES FROM WANDA

Several people have asked why I think Viola didn't get back in her car and finish her trip [after spending the night in jail]. But I think for the first time, her mind wasn't on business. Besides being physically unwell, I believe losing at court was a blow to her pride. So she turned back, came home. I remember how angry my father was when he saw how she had been abused. He was very protective of Viola and insisted she visit the family doctor, Dr. Waddell. He was a Black physician from the West Indies, living and working in Halifax, but because of his skin color, he was not allowed to practice at the local hospital. Dr. Waddell was horrified by Viola's injuries and told her she should see a lawyer. He even wrote several letters to the federal government in Ottawa about what had happened to Viola at the Roseland Theatre.

seven

ONE SINGLE CENT

Everything in the jail cell was gray. Viola even felt gray. But she refused to show it. Instead she pulled on her white gloves. Keeping her back perfectly straight, she sat down on the bed in the corner. She stayed up all night, going through her appointment book, planning the week ahead.

The following day Viola was brought to court. The usher, cashier, Henry and the police officer were already there. They lied, arguing that Viola had bought an upstairs ticket and then hadn't sat in the correct place. She was accused of not paying the difference in **tax** for the downstairs ticket—a single penny.

Viola didn't have a lawyer. She hadn't even been allowed to make a phone call. Without any help, Viola realized she would have to argue her own case. In a firm, quiet voice, Viola told them what had happened. She explained that she had tried to pay the correct price. "I offered," she said. "It was refused."

ONE CENT

Nobody believed her. The judge declared Viola guilty of not paying the one cent in tax. She was fined $20. On top of this, she was charged an extra $6 to pay for Henry's court fees. Twenty-six dollars may not seem like a lot, but it would be equal to $350 today. If she didn't pay the fine, she would spend 30 days in jail. Later Viola said she would rather have spent the time in jail.

But she felt responsible for her students at the Desmond School of Beauty Culture.

Throughout the trial, no one said anything about the color of Viola's skin. They only argued about the one cent of tax. But everyone knew the real reason Viola was blamed. She was furious as she walked out of the courtroom. She returned to the service station to get her car. Instead of going on to Sydney, she turned around and drove back to Halifax.

STRIDE TOWARD FREEDOM

When Viola got home, she went to see her best friend, Pearleen Oliver. Pearleen was appalled to see the bruises on Viola's body. "Oh dear God, Viola, what did they do to you?" she asked.

Pearleen was no stranger to racism. She had experienced it firsthand and helped others fight for equal rights. She encouraged

BLACK WOMEN FIGHT BACK

Black women played a significant role as defenders of civil rights in their communities. They organized boycotts of stores that would not hire Black employees and offered arts, music and literature programs to students in underfunded Black schools. Black church women placed pressure on their local hospitals to admit Black women into their nursing programs, helping them secure better-paying jobs. When a theater in Winnipeg scheduled regular showings of a movie called *The Clansman,* Black women staged a protest outside the theater. They argued against the film's racist content. The theater ended the movie's run sooner than planned.

Viola to get a lawyer and appeal the court's ruling. People can request an appeal in a higher court if they feel a decision was unfair.

Viola thought about this. She had come up against discrimination all her life. Because of her race, she had been refused training, had taught only in segregated schools and had frequently encountered racism in the beauty business.

She'd just wanted to see a movie. Now she was injured and had spent a whole night in jail. Viola made up her mind. Black people ought to have the same rights as white people. She would hire a lawyer and fight back.

PEARLEEN OLIVER

Dr. Pearleen Oliver was a community leader and civil rights activist. In the 1940s and '50s she fought for equal opportunities in education and employment for Black people. In 1947 she successfully campaigned to get Black women admitted to nursing schools in Canada. Together with her husband, Rev. Dr. William P. Oliver, she cofounded the Nova Scotia Association for the Advancement of Coloured People (NSAACP).

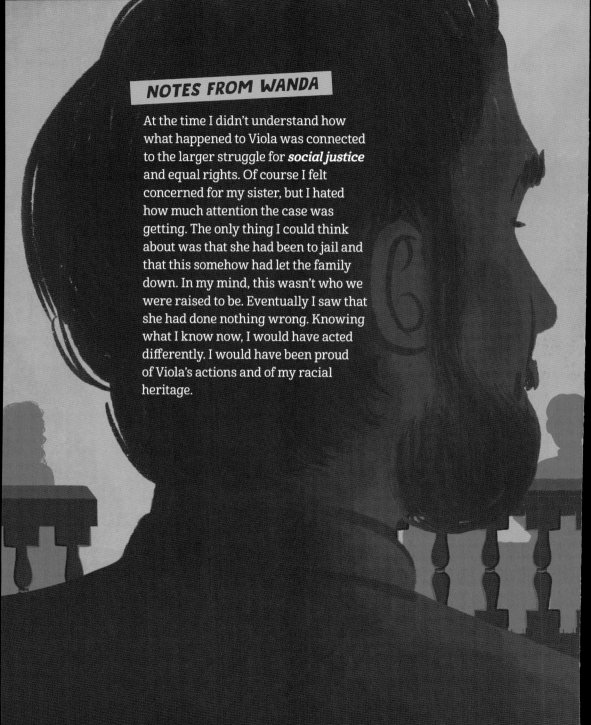

NOTES FROM WANDA

At the time I didn't understand how what happened to Viola was connected to the larger struggle for *social justice* and equal rights. Of course I felt concerned for my sister, but I hated how much attention the case was getting. The only thing I could think about was that she had been to jail and that this somehow had let the family down. In my mind, this wasn't who we were raised to be. Eventually I saw that she had done nothing wrong. Knowing what I know now, I would have acted differently. I would have been proud of Viola's actions and of my racial heritage.

eight

TAKING A STAND

Viola would need the support of the entire Black community if she was going to win her appeal. Pearleen convinced the Nova Scotia Association for the Advancement of Coloured People (NSAACP) to accept Viola's case. A Viola Desmond Court Fund was created. This would help cover the cost for Viola to hire a lawyer and make her appeal.

Not everyone supported Viola. Her husband, Jack, thought trying to seek justice would only stir up trouble. He refused to go with her to court. And Viola's sister Wanda hated the attention the case was getting. She felt embarrassed that her sister had been sent to jail.

Besides Pearleen, Viola only had one other person in her corner. Carrie Best, Viola's friend and customer at the salon,

CARRIE BEST AND *THE CLARION*

Carrie Best was a civil rights activist and journalist. She was the owner of *The Clarion*, one of the first Black-owned Nova Scotia newspapers. The newspaper focused on issues of discrimination and the lives of Black Nova Scotians. Just like Viola, Carrie had experienced racial segregation at the Roseland Theatre. In 1941 she was turned out of the theater for trying to take a seat in the downstairs section. She took the matter to court, but her case was ultimately unsuccessful. In 1979 Carrie became an Officer of the Order of Canada, and she was awarded the Order of Nova Scotia in 2002 for her commitment to racial equality and social justice.

lived in New Glasgow and ran *The Clarion* newspaper. She wrote a front-page article about what had happened to Viola, calling it a "disgraceful incident." She urged people to help raise money for the Viola Desmond Court Fund.

TELLING HER STORY

As word spread, more people started to get angry about the way Viola had been treated. Donations from people, both Black and white, poured in from across the province. They wanted to support Viola and help end discrimination against Black Canadians.

Pearleen's husband, William, suggested Viola hire his friend and lawyer Frederick William Bissett. Frederick felt Viola had

NOVA SCOTIA ASSOCIATION FOR THE ADVANCEMENT OF COLOURED PEOPLE (NSAACP)

Founded in 1945 by William and Pearleen Oliver and seven other Black leaders, the NSAACP was a civil rights group located at the Cornwallis Street Baptist Church in Halifax. Their goal was to improve the lives of Black Nova Scotians by eliminating racial discrimination in education, housing and employment. The organization had 500 members and several locations throughout Nova Scotia.

a strong case. She was a hard-working and successful entrepreneur. She was also a respectable married woman who had the support of her community. Viola had to make her plea in front of the Nova Scotia Supreme Court. Frederick assured Viola there was "no evidence to support" her **conviction**. She had asked for a downstairs ticket and offered to

MAKING WAVES

In the 1960s Black former senator Calvin Ruck was denied a haircut at a barbershop in Shearwater, Nova Scotia. Calvin and his family sat in the shop and refused to leave. The owner was so embarrassed that he eventually cut Calvin's hair.

pay the difference in cost. He laid charges against Henry MacNeil, the manager of the Roseland, for illegally removing Viola from the theater and injuring her in the process.

Viola was nervous about going to court. But this time she had her lawyer and Carrie Best accompanying her. On March 13, 1947, they appeared before four Supreme Court judges. Carrie said she "watched breathlessly as Mr. Bissett argued his appeal...hoping against hope that justice will not be blind." But the judges didn't listen. They claimed Frederick had waited too long to ask for an appeal. Viola's conviction remained.

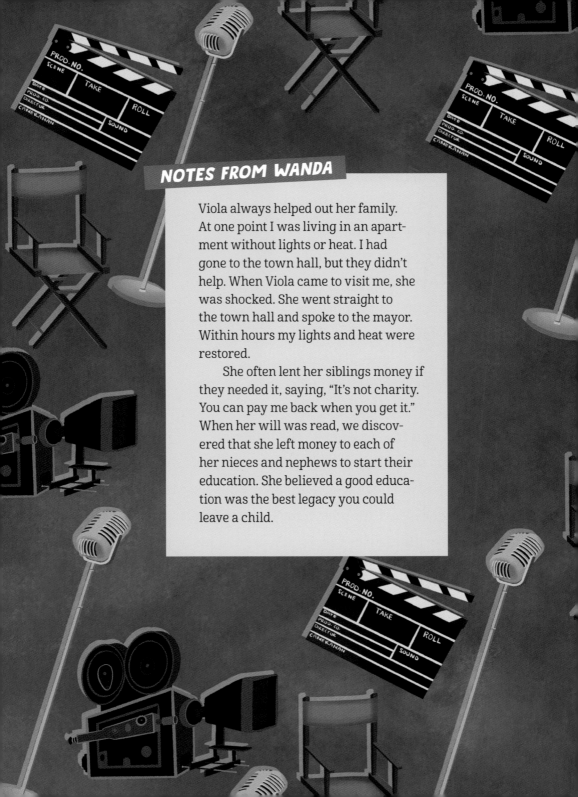

NOTES FROM WANDA

Viola always helped out her family. At one point I was living in an apartment without lights or heat. I had gone to the town hall, but they didn't help. When Viola came to visit me, she was shocked. She went straight to the town hall and spoke to the mayor. Within hours my lights and heat were restored.

She often lent her siblings money if they needed it, saying, "It's not charity. You can pay me back when you get it." When her will was read, we discovered that she left money to each of her nieces and nephews to start their education. She believed a good education was the best legacy you could leave a child.

nine

MOVING ON

A TIME FOR CHANGE

In Canada the fight to end racial segregation happened gradually from province to province. In Ontario Hugh Burnett, a Black World War II veteran, fought against discrimination after being refused service in a café in his hometown of Dresden. Together with other Black community members, Hugh formed the National Unity Association (NUA) in 1948. The NUA gained the support of other human rights activists who petitioned the Ontario government to outlaw discrimination in the province. Their actions resulted in the creation of *anti-segregation laws* in Ontario.

When Viola appeared at the Supreme Court, once again no one mentioned anything about her race. No one argued against the Roseland Theatre's decision to enforce segregated seating. Only one judge, Justice Hall, recognized that the verdict against Viola was unfair. He knew the case wasn't about the one cent of tax. It was about keeping Black people separate from white people.

Viola was shocked. She had always believed that if she worked hard, she would prevail. It had taken a lot of courage for her to stand up against discrimination. The decision left her bitterly disappointed. Her lawyer, Frederick Bissett, felt horrible that he had let Viola down. So he did the only thing he could think of. He donated his legal fees for the case to the Nova Scotia Association for the Advancement of Coloured People (NSAACP).

Both the NSAACP and *The Clarion* wanted Viola to keep fighting. She had become an inspiration to other Black people in her community. They wanted her to tell her story and support the struggle for civil rights. But Viola didn't want to continue protesting. She knew she'd been unfairly judged because she was Black. It didn't matter that she was a respected business-woman. All they saw was the color of her skin.

Things had also become difficult between Viola and Jack. He hated the publicity from the case and didn't like how it threw Viola into the spotlight. They continued to grow further apart until they separated in 1954.

NEW DIRECTIONS

After Viola lost her case, she went to her father to ask for advice. James told her she had gone as far as she could. He thought it was time to put her experience in court behind her. She had a responsibility to her customers and, in particular, her students.

So Viola got back to work. That year she graduated her second class of 15 students from the Desmond School of Beauty Culture. She continued to supply customers with beauty products and sold them around the province. Viola still dreamed of expanding her business throughout the country.

WOMEN UNITED

In 1954 the Prince Edward Hotel in Windsor, Ontario, denied Black civil rights activist Mary McLeod Bethune a room. She and First Lady Eleanor Roosevelt had been invited to speak the next day at Windsor's annual *Emancipation* Day celebration. The First Lady was given a room, but she refused to take it. Instead both women decided to stay in Detroit for the night.

But while she had been busy in court, other businesses had started to sell specialized products for Black people. In 1949 Mirror Tone Hair Products came out with a line of products that were advertised in *The Clarion*. Larger department stores began to sell cosmetics for Black women all across Canada. Viola worked hard to increase sales. But with such competition, the struggle to grow her brand became impossible. She closed Vi's Studio of Beauty Culture in 1955.

But Viola didn't give up.

She decided to apply her business skills in a different area. Following the separation from her husband, Viola moved to Montreal and then to New York City, where she went to business

college and eventually became an entertainment agent. Viola worked with singers and actors to help them find work. Her business was just about to take off. But on February 7, 1965, at just 50 years old, she died suddenly of internal bleeding, in her Harlem apartment.

There wasn't one word in her obituary about her struggle against discrimination at the Roseland Theatre. Nearly 20 years had passed since then, and many thought her heroic stand against racism was forgotten.

But Viola's story doesn't end here.

ten

VIOLA'S LEGACY

NOTES FROM WANDA

I think of Viola almost every day. It pains me that she did not live to see the celebration of her achievements. To know all that she has done for us. But the new $10 bill serves as a constant reminder of her actions in the struggle for equal rights. Now more people will tell her story. They will remember the brave actions of a woman taken out of a movie theater in Canada because she refused to leave the whites-only section. Thinking about this helps keep Viola's memory alive. Because of her, we can look back on the days when racism and intolerance were more accepted and see how far we have come.

Viola's quiet act of defiance at the Roseland Theatre inspired the Black community and united them in protest. Her actions helped raise awareness and encouraged others to resist discrimination.

Spurred on by Viola's courage, *The Clarion* and the Nova Scotia Association for the Advancement of Coloured People (NSAACP) continued to seek justice. Remembering Viola's brave struggle, William Oliver said, "Neither before or since has there been such an aggressive effort to obtain rights. The people arose as one and with one voice."

Viola never lived to see Black people receive equal rights. But her act of bravery revealed the anger of the Black community and the need for change. They were no longer willing to tolerate life as second-class citizens. Her actions brought about remarkable changes. In 1959 the Nova Scotia government passed the Fair Accommodation Practices Act. This meant Black people had to be treated equally in public places such as hotels, restaurants and theaters. The Nova Scotia Human Rights Act followed in 1963, making racial discrimination against the law. Black people now had equal rights at work and when buying a home, and received equal pay.

The fight for civil rights grew stronger throughout the 1960s and '70s. Black organizations helped improve housing, education and job opportunities. In 1977 the Canadian Human Rights Act was introduced, and it removed any unfair rules

THE MARCH ON WASHINGTON

On August 28, 1963, a crowd of 250,000 people gathered in front of the Lincoln Memorial in Washington, DC. The march rallied Black Americans to stand up against the political and social injustice they still faced a century after emancipation. The march is best remembered for Martin Luther King Jr.'s speech, "I Have a Dream." This prompted the creation of the Civil Rights Act of 1964, prohibiting discrimination on the basis of race.

that discriminated against Black Canadians. It was now law that Black people receive the same rights as white people.

SETTING THE RECORD STRAIGHT

History shows that Viola's fight against racism signified a turning point in the struggle for civil rights. But she also left a personal legacy. Viola had a lifelong influence on the women who attended the Desmond School of Beauty Culture. Former students Rose Gannon, Rachel Kane, Geraldine Hunter and Bernadine Bishop became successful beauticians who started their own businesses in Nova Scotia and beyond. Several other students remember her as an independent and modern woman who championed women's rights.

But it was her sister Wanda who brought her story to the world.

When Wanda was younger, she was embarrassed that her sister had been sent to jail. But as she grew older, she realized

Viola had not done anything wrong. She had been brave. Viola had confronted racism and stood up for Black people's rights. Now Wanda felt proud.

She started to tell Viola's story. She gave interviews, presented at universities and spoke to children in schools. It felt good to talk about Viola's bravery and the importance of taking a stand.

Then Wanda heard that the Nova Scotia government was considering a free pardon for Viola. Newspapers, magazines and radio stations called for interviews. Once again Viola was in the spotlight. Only this time, she was being celebrated.

THE HONORABLE DR. MAYANN FRANCIS

Mayann Francis was Canada's first Black female lieutenant governor. She initially heard about Viola Desmond's story through a friend who had been inspired by Viola to start her own cosmetics business. Mayann attributes her success to all the women like Viola, who fought peacefully for justice and equality for Black Canadians.

On April 15, 2010, Nova Scotia premier Darrell Dexter apologized to Viola's family and the entire Black community in Nova Scotia. Lieutenant Governor Mayann Francis exercised the Royal Prerogative of Mercy to grant a free pardon declaring Viola innocent. She had never been guilty of any crime, and "the treatment she received...was not fair." Viola is the first Canadian to receive a pardon after her death.

RIGHTING A WRONG

Following the pardon, it was decided that Viola's struggle to create an equal society deserved greater recognition. So on March 8, 2018, she became the first Black woman to appear alone on Canadian paper money. The $10 bill was unveiled by the Bank of Canada at the Halifax Central Library. Behind her portrait is a map of Halifax's North End, including Gottingen Street, where she had her beauty salon.

This tribute reminds us all of the quiet resistance of one woman who became a symbol of courage to the entire nation. Her story shows us that change can begin with a small act of bravery. Strong and determined, Viola stood up against injustice and changed the course of history.

TIME LINE

JULY 6, 1914—Viola is born in Halifax, Nova Scotia

JULY 1936—Receives training at the Field Beauty Culture School in Montreal and marries Jack Desmond

SEPTEMBER 1937—Opens Vi's Studio of Beauty Culture in Halifax

1939—Attends Apex College of Beauty Culture and Hairdressing in Atlantic City

1941—Completes an *apprenticeship* at the Louis Feder Advanced Hair Styling Studio in New York City

1944—Opens the Desmond School of Beauty Culture in Halifax

NOVEMBER 8, 1946—Arrested at the Roseland Theatre in New Glasgow, Nova Scotia

NOVEMBER 9, 1946—Taken to court and found guilty of not paying one cent in tax

MARCH 13, 1947—Nova Scotia Supreme Court dismisses her appeal

1954—Moves to Montreal and takes a course in business

1955—Moves to New York City and becomes an entertainment agent

FEBRUARY 7, 1965—Dies in her apartment in New York City

APRIL 15, 2010—Granted a full pardon from the government of Nova Scotia

FEBRUARY 1, 2012—Appears on a commemorative stamp issued by Canada Post

JULY 7, 2016—A Halifax harbor ferry bearing her name is launched

NOVEMBER 15, 2017—Inducted into Canada's Walk of Fame

JANUARY 12, 2018—Declared a National Historic Person

MARCH 8, 2018—Viola is featured on the $10 bill. She is the first Black Canadian woman to appear alone on a banknote.

GLOSSARY

anti-segregation laws—rules that made it illegal to restrict Black people to certain areas or separate institutions

apprenticeship—job training in which someone learns an art or skill by studying under a master of that trade

beautician—someone who provides many types of beauty treatments, from hairstyling to makeup application

civil rights movement—the organized fight to achieve equality for African Americans, which occurred between the mid-1950s and late 1960s. The rights of a country's citizens are called *civil rights*.

conviction—the act of finding a person guilty of a crime

dreadlocks—a hairstyle featuring ropelike strands of hair, formed by braiding or twisting

emancipation—freedom from the control or restraint of others

entrepreneurs—people who set up and manage their own businesses

equal rights—having the same access to education, housing and healthcare no matter your race, ethnic background, religion or gender

Great Depression—a massive economic decline lasting from 1929 to 1939 during which many people lost their jobs and became homeless

integrate—unite; eliminate the separation of people from different racial backgrounds

munitions—military weapons and ammunition

pardon—an official act that frees a person from a conviction

pioneer—a person who is the first to do something, opening the way for others to follow

racial segregation—separating people on the basis of their race

racism—unfair treatment of people based on the color of their skin

scalp lesions—sores that may itch or bleed and cause hair to fall out

slavery—the practice of people "owning" others and forcing them to work for them

social justice—fairness in all aspects of society, from healthcare to housing, for all people no matter their race, age, gender, religion or sexuality

tax—money people must pay to the government for things like schools and roads

RESOURCES

Print

Cavallo, Francesca, and Elena Favilli. *Good Night Stories for Rebel Girls: 100 Tales of Extraordinary Women*. Rebels Girls, 2016.

Howden, Sarah. *5-Minute Stories for Fearless Girls*. HarperCollins, 2018.

MacLeod, Elizabeth. *Canadian Women Now and Then: More than 100 Stories of Fearless Trailblazers*. Kids Can Press, 2020.

MacLeod, Elizabeth. *Scholastic Canada Biography: Meet Viola Desmond*. Scholastic Canada, 2018.

Moyer, Naomi M. *Black Women Who Dared*. Second Story Press, 2018.

Petry, Ann. *Harriet Tubman: Conductor on the Underground Railroad*. Revised edition. Amistad, 2018.

Shetterly, Margot Lee. *Hidden Figures: Young Readers' Edition*. HarperCollins, 2016.

Warner, Jody Nyasha. *Viola Desmond Won't Be Budged*. Groundwood Books, 2018.

Online

"Canada's Great Women." Canada's History, January 8, 2016: canadashistory.ca/explore/women/canada-s-great-women

Coren, Ashleigh D., Meredith Holmgren, Anya Montiel and Sara Cohen. "Twelve Black Women to Know." Smithsonian American Women's History Museum: womenshistory.si.edu/stories/2021/02/twelve-black-women-know

"How Did Black History Month Come to Be?" CBC Kids, January 31, 2022: cbc.ca/kids/articles/all-about-black-history-month

Kayak: Canada's History Magazine for Kids, Special 2022 Edition. Canada's History Society: canadashistory.ca/education/kayak-in-the-classroom/black-history/black-history-educational-package

"One Woman's Resistance: Viola Desmond's Story." Canadian Museum for Human Rights: humanrights.ca/story/one-womans-resistance

"Women in Canadian History" collection, *Canadian Encyclopedia*: thecanadianencyclopedia.ca/en/collection/women-in-canada

ACKNOWLEDGMENTS

I am over the moon that you are holding the first chapter book about Viola Desmond in your hands right now. I learned so much as I researched the life of this remarkable woman and listened to stories that ultimately gave me the inspiration for this book. But none of this would have been possible without the many wonderful people who work behind the scenes.

First, I am deeply grateful to Wanda Robson, whose grace and generosity know no bounds. Sharing her personal experiences about life as a Black woman in Canada and treasured memories of her beloved sister helped bring this extraordinary woman to life. Wanda's unrelenting mission to remind the world of Viola's quiet act of courage is the reason we celebrate Viola Desmond today. When Viola needed a hero, that's who Wanda became.

Boundless thanks to Joe Robson, who served as an indefatigable fact-checker and essential source of information.

I'm deeply indebted to the amazing Graham Reynolds for his invaluable advice and tireless support. Graham is Professor Emeritus of history and the Viola Desmond Chair at Cape Breton University. His inspiring work has raised awareness about the history of Black people in Canada and their struggle for racial equality. His publications on the history of racial segregation in Canada have served as vital sources of information in the creation of this book.

Thank you to everyone at Orca Book Publishers who helped me so much. Special thanks to Kirstie Hudson for your clever and thoughtful edits; to Rachel Page—you are a fantastic designer; and Chelsea Charles, for being the best illustrator I could ever imagine.

Thanks to my incredible family: my grandmother, Agnes, for her strength and encouragement; my dad, for a lifetime of love and support; and my mother, a fellow amazing woman who always lifts me up.

The biggest thank-you to my husband, Bas, for standing by me through every struggle and success. And finally, to Isla, Rose and Rhys, for your never-ending love and for always making me proud.

RACHEL KEHOE is a nonfiction writer who has dreamed of writing books about fierce females all her life. She writes for *Muse* and *Faces* magazines and has also published several nonfiction books for kids on topics such as climate change, energy technology, artificial intelligence and mental health awareness. Rachel is an avid reader, traveler and photographer who has worked in Australia, Europe and Asia. When she isn't writing, Rachel is researching new destinations for her family to explore. She lives in Burlington, Ontario.

The late **WANDA ROBSON** was a well-known storyteller, author, community activist and unceasing crusader in seeking justice for her older sister Viola Desmond, who was wrongly arrested in 1946 for sitting in the "white only" section of the Roseland Theatre in New Glasgow, Nova Scotia. In 2010 she published *Sister to Courage: Stories from the World of Viola Desmond*. Wanda was a longtime resident of North Sydney, Nova Scotia, where she lived with her husband, Joe, until she passed away in 2022.

CHELSEA CHARLES is an illustrator who resides in Brampton, Ontario, and received her BAA in illustration from Sheridan College. She creates her illustrations through a combination of digital and traditional mediums.

CHANGEMAKERS

Inspiring the activist in all of us

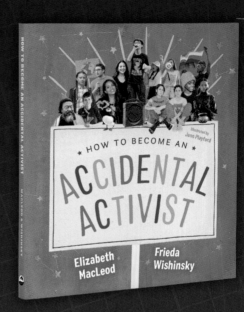

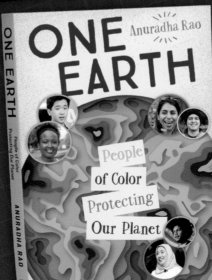

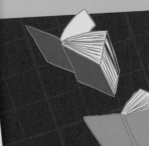